AMBIVALENCE

- A poetic journey to introspect, discover, and grow as an adult.

Shahzneen Patel

Winner of the 21st Century Emily Dickinson Award

BookLeaf Publishing

India | USA | UK

Presentation by *BookLeaf Publishing*

Web: www.bookleafpub.com

E-mail: info@bookleafpub.com

ISBN: 9789367397282

First edition 2025

Disclaimer

The contents of this book are general in nature. This book is not to be used as a substitute for examination, diagnosis, treatment, or advice from a trained professional.

Readers are advised to seek professional help while dealing with mental health, behavioural, psychological, or psychiatric issues, including but not limited to depression.

The views and opinions expressed in this book are those of the author and reflect her own understanding of real life scenarios and people's emotions. They do not represent the views or opinions of any other person.

The objective of this book is not to hurt any sentiments, insult, or cause offence to any particular person, group, or community, including those of any caste, religion, region, linguistic background, or sexual identity.

Neither the author nor the publisher shall be liable for any loss, harm, or damage that may result from the contents of this book.

Bookleaf Ananda

Shahzneen Patel is an instructional designer and a management consultant professional with an exemplary background in creating engaging and learner-centric content.

She has successfully designed and implemented curricula for over 4,000 learners, enhancing learning outcomes and skill acquisition across various postgraduate, management, leadership, and corporate customised programs.

Her expertise spans diverse industries, including retail, consumer goods, EdTech, and consulting, with successful collaborations across the Asia-Pacific and Middle East regions.

Shahzneen's passion lies in making learning precise, clear, and accessible, enabling individuals to upskill and grow. Her mission is simple yet powerful: to make learning effortless, engaging, and impactful.

By crafting content that is crisp, clear, and easy to grasp, she helps others learn, upskill, and grow.

Every opportunity becomes a chance not only to master new concepts but also to elevate her professional journey, honing her skills as an instructional designer.

But her passion doesn't stop there. She's now channeling her creativity into writing a book that delves into the fascinating world of human emotions—how we perceive them and how they shape our lives.

Drawing from her own observations, she invites readers to embrace their authentic selves and encourages them to unlock their emotional potential.

Through this book, she's on a mission to inspire others to live fully and be unapologetically themselves.

Acknowledgement

Creating Ambivalence has been a journey of introspection, discovery, and profound personal growth. This book would not have been possible without the unwavering support, encouragement, and inspiration of many incredible individuals.

First and foremost, I extend my deepest gratitude to my family. Your steadfast belief in me became the foundation upon which this book was built. Your patience, understanding, and love gave me the strength to explore the complexities of human emotion and experience with honesty and depth.

To my friends and loved ones, thank you for your honest feedback, insightful discussions, and endless encouragement. Your perspectives have enriched this narrative and allowed me to see the many facets of Ambivalence in new and profound ways.

To my readers, thank you for embarking on this journey with me. Your openness to exploring the intricate and often challenging emotions within these pages is what gives Ambivalence its true purpose. I hope these stories resonate with you, offering solace, reflection, and a deeper connection to our shared human experience.

Lastly, I want to acknowledge all those whose stories of triumph and struggle have inspired the tales within these pages. Your courage and resilience are the heart of "Ambivalence." It is through your experiences that the essence of this book came to life, reminding us all of the beauty and complexity of the human condition.

With heartfelt gratitude,
Shahzneen Patel

Contents

Author's Note

In a world filled with constant change and relentless motion, the complexities of our inner lives often remain unnoticed, unspoken, and unexamined. Ambivalence, through its poems, seeks to illuminate these hidden depths, weaving together a nuanced tapestry of real-life experiences and the everyday challenges that shape our existence. More than just a collection of stories, this book is a compelling narrative that captures the essence of human uncertainty - of the inner conflicts and contradictions that reside within us all.

Through vivid and empathetic storytelling, Ambivalence, through its poems, seeks to explore the intricate emotional landscapes that we navigate daily. It reflects the delicate balance we strive for, amidst the unpredictability of life. Each poem serves as a window into the soul, revealing how our emotions intertwine, clash, and coalesce as we journey through the highs and lows of our personal and shared experiences.

In writing Ambivalence, my goal was to offer a reflection on the human condition that resonates deeply with each reader. By capturing the trials and triumphs that define us, this book aims to provide a mirror to our own uncertainties, fears, and hopes. It is an exploration of how we reconcile our internal contradictions and find meaning and clarity in the midst of chaos.

This book is dedicated to those who embrace their inner ambivalence, who understand that life's richness comes from its complexity and unpredictability. May Ambivalence bring you solace, insight, and a renewed appreciation for the beautifully intricate, ever evolving journey we all share.

"A bad system will beat a good person every time."

- W. Edwards Deming

Noise

A working lady with a keen mind,
Hard work and experience, she refined,
Aiming to be the best, you'll find.

Her learning curve was steep,
Lightening-fast grasp of subject, made others
weep,
Swift execution, she dove deep,
Superstar dreams, ambitions leaped.

But envy whispered among peers,
Emerging insecurities, ignited fears,
Reservations against skills, stoked by jeers,
Undermined efforts, drowned in tears.

Yet she manoeuvred the path with grace,
Burning the midnight oil, to prove her place,
And negativity continued its relentless chase.

Intimidated and stressed in tow,
A dim spirit, yet she continued her show,
Lost in shadows, her confidence stole.

Despite her strive, her performance waned,
A downward spiral, her efforts strained,
They rejoiced, their victory feigned,
Leaving her heart heavy, her will drained.

Ready to heal, not to fall apart,
Determined to make a fresh start,
She'll rise again, a brand new chart.

"Though you've built a new life, you'll
always have a special place in my heart, and
I'll always be here to hold your hand, even if
it's from afar."

- A mother

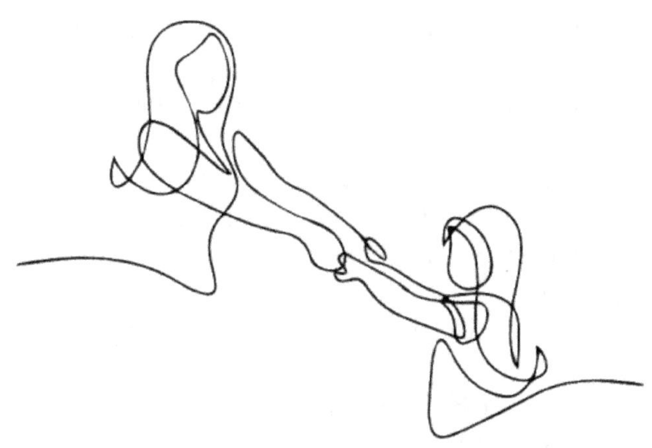

Endless

A house brimming with laughter, songs,
Mother counts days, where silence belongs.
Her daughter, once nestled close with care,
Now married, leaving memories to share.

She gave her heart, soul, every beat,
In her daughter's eyes, life felt complete.
A teacher, friend, guide for life, in all,
Lifted her child, each time she would fall.

Overprotective, yet wishing the best,
Worried about her crowd, her path, her rest,
Mild fevers, small colds, brought concern to her eyes,
Love wrapped in caution, beneath open skies.

Now each day feels different, a void to fill,
Tea once shared now sits still.
She calls her, bridging the divide,
Rejoices in visits, heart filled with pride.

Loneliness creeps in, a shadow stark,
Love misunderstood, left in the dark.
But she's resilient, a strong woman still,
Decides to learn, has dreams to fulfill.

Skills to master, paths to tread,
A pillar, though silent tears are shed.
She'll always be the rock,
For every storm, she's the door to knock.

Her heart aches, yet she wears a brave face,
Finding new joy, filling empty space.
She knows though they're apart,
A mother's love is endless, an unbreakable part.

"In the early days of marriage, joy precedes the act. Tragically, as the years go by joy can be severed from the act until finally, the act itself is no more. This ought not to be. Over time it is the companionship that brings joy, and service is the natural outworking of the joy of commitment. Failure to act kills it."

- Ravi Zacharias

Teething

In the early days of wedded bliss,
They faced some bumps they couldn't miss.
With varied views on love's embrace,
Their hearts would often find their place.

Romance to them meant different things,
From simple joys to grander rings.
Moments of laughter, pure delight,
Could quickly turn to tears at night.

Conversations filled with cheer,
Sometimes led to moments drear.
Joyful banter, light and free,
Could twist to doubt and unease.

Intimacy, a subtle art,
Where two souls played their part.
Passionate nights with stars aglow,
Could fade to silent tears below.

Meals at home, a dance of taste,
With flavors neither would erase.
Shared delight in culinary fun,
Could turn to grumbles, moods undone.

Sleep routines, a varied song,
Each found solace all night long.
Harmony in dreams, serene,
Could shift to restless nights unseen.

Household chores, a shared task,
In unity, they'd often bask.
Togetherness brought pride and glee,
But also spats and muttered pleas.

Family ties, a web so fine,
Each would blend their kin divine.
Warm gatherings, love's embrace,
Could lead to tension, anxious face.

Handling expenses, a careful tread,
With thoughtful plans and words unsaid.
Contentment in a balanced day,
Could turn to stress, bills to pay.

Through every challenge, big and small,
Their love would rise above it all.
For in each difference, they would see,
The strength of their unity.

Hand in hand, through joy and strife,
They crafted their shared life.
In every step, they'd come to know,
Their love was meant to grow.

Emotions flowed, a vivid stream,
From rage to peace, to every dream.
In the tapestry of married life,
They found their way through love and strife.

"Survival can be summed up in three words
– never give up. That's the heart of it really.
Just keep trying."

- Bear Grylls

Survival

In the world of modern stride,
The art of living slips aside.
A frantic race to rise and thrive,
Yet bound in chains, we barely survive.

We burn in effort, day by day,
A pressure cooker, led astray.
Our minds, once sharp, now frail and weak,
In roles we built, we seldom speak.

Emotions tossed, we lose our way,
In endless tasks that steal the day.
The ones we love, pushed aside,
As we march on, swallowed by pride.

The simple joys drift out of sight,
Replaced by noise, by endless fight.
Self-worth dissolves in waves of doubt,
Confidence, a drought throughout.

Money reigns, this frantic chase,
Everywhere, a frantic pace.
Bills and rent, the weight we bear,
Children's needs, constant care.

Each dime we spend, with trembling hand,
In a world that worships time's demand.
Infrastructure rises, tall and grand,
Yet where's the heart beneath the land?

Material gains, a fleeting high,
Leave us empty, questioning why.
True happiness, a dream so far,
Lost in the rush, beneath each star.

We've built a world of stone and steel,
Yet deep inside, we never heal.
In striving hard to reach the peak,
We've forgotten how to truly seek.

Stress and anger, constant friends,
Fill our lives with silent ends.
We've lost the way to love ourselves,
Trapped in a race that never helps.

Let's pause, breathe, and start anew,
Reclaim life, from what we knew.
Find joy in moments, large and small,
And cherish what we have, after all.

For in the end, it's love we seek,
Not the pace that leaves us weak.
It's love and grace, a steady guide,
That lets us live, and lets us glide.

"It's all about finding the calm in the chaos."

- Donna Karen

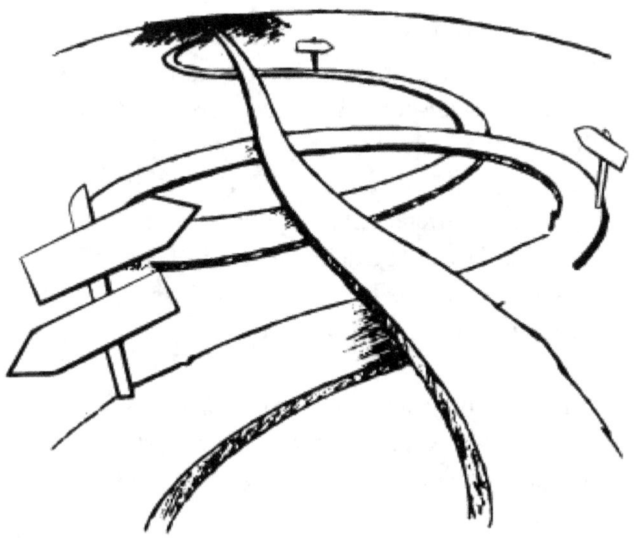

Commotion

A tapestry of days, she threads her life,
Every moment, a thread, a strife.
Juggling duties, roles are a sharp knife,
Balancing the chaos in her life.

At work, adrift in a crowded zone,
Boss's nagging, turns her heart to stone.
Loneliness whispers, colleagues surround,
She feels isolated in this battleground.

At home, a different play unfolds,
A husband's touch, distant and cold.
Misunderstandings brew in silence deep,
Different dreams in a marriage to keep.

Parents on both sides, a balancing act,
Their well-being, a vow she won't retract.
A house to manage, every corner her realm,
In every detail, she must overwhelm.

Her books and studies, ambitions bright,
Fade in the shadows of her daily fight.
Social ties fray, as time slips away,
Chores and duties dictate her day.

Yet through it all, she must appear fair,
Picture-perfect, beauty without a care.
Doubt creeps in, a shadow on her wall,
"Am I enough?" as minor errors call.

Survival, her mantra, calm out of reach,
In chaos, life's lessons continue to teach.
She doubts her path in this quest,
Yet her heart strives to do the best.

Silence in the storm, her strength,
A warrior's grace, enduring at length.
Though she feels nothing is going well,
In her perseverance, a true story dwells.

"Dreams don't work unless you do."

- John C. Maxwell

Anchor

They brought life forth and new,
A child beneath skies, streaked in dusky hue.
Weathered hands, cradled with tender grace,
Love entwined in a soft and sacred space.

From dawn to dusk, a heavy heart bears,
The weight of care, a load so hard to share.
Grandparents fragile, in time's gentle fold,
Once strong parents, now silent and cold.

Young child, with dreams yet undefined,
Juggling life's demands, with weight confined.
In books and lessons, seeking knowledge bright,
Bound by duty, her soul tugs through the night.

Eyes should wander, and roam with glee,
Turned to faces worn, by love and duty's plea.
Youth's adventures whisper, fading slight,
But the blood and care ties hold her tight.

An uncertain future, paths stretch wide,
A life not yet hers, by family's need she's tied.
Between her dreams and ones holds so dear,
She treads a fragile line, heart gripped by fear.

In stolen moments, she dares to dream,
To carve a space, amidst the endless grieve.
Yet, in the quiet, doubts begin to creep,
What if dreams are too far to reach, too deep?

Balancing self and duty, a dance so frail,
To honor all that came, yet let her spirit sail.
In her hands, a legacy so precious and dear,
But her heart, a future that is hers to steer.

May strength and wisdom guide in the dark,
To find her way, to ignite her spark.
Though her journey is hard, her heart remains true,
A soul of love and duty, enduring through.

"When it becomes really impossible to get
away and sleep, then the will to live
evaporates of its own accord."

- Louis-Ferdinand Céline

Insomnia

In the night's stillness, a mind seeks peace,
Yet sleep eludes, a quiet thief.
A heart, soft and steady, aches for rest,
But the hours unravel, an endless test.

Eyes locked on screens, flickering bright,
Hoping for weariness to take its flight.
The rhythm of videos, a numbing lullaby,
But morning comes with a heavy sigh.

The sun ascends, casting light anew,
Yet the weight of tiredness clouds the view.
A promise made, to rise, to grow,
But energy wanes, too far to go.

A day derailed, a schedule askew,
The glow of productivity fades from view.
Guilt creeps closer, its shadow near,
Of wasted hours, of dreams unclear.

Each night, a vow to break the chain,
To reclaim rest, to ease the strain.
But habits, deep-rooted, tighten their hold,
The cycle repeats, growing old.

A peaceful mind, yet restless still,
A silent struggle, an aching will.
To find the way to quiet sleep,
A promise made, a vow to keep.

May strength be found in twilight's hours,
To shift the tide, reclaim lost powers.
For peaceful hearts, though worn, deserve,
To rest, to heal, to face the curve.

"You're never as good as everyone tells you
when you win, and you're never as bad as
they say when you lose."

- Lou Holtz

Still

In the quiet shadows, I lie alone,
Wrapped in thoughts, a heart of stone.
Past echoes whisper, relentless and stark,
From personal wounds and professional marks.

The world suggests, with voices loud,
Endless paths to lift the shroud.
Yet their advice, a hollow call,
Only deepens this solitary wall.

They speak of triumphs, their own grand tales,
With no space for my pain's details.
Their pride a barrier, their empathy lost,
Leaving me adrift, bearing the cost.

I feel unseen, a ghost in the tide,
My struggles dismissed, my truth set aside.
A boss's disdain, a family's blind gaze,
Trivializing my battles, trapped in a haze.

Doubt creeps in, an insidious thief,
Undermining my confidence, eroding belief.
Even in stillness, the storm inside rages,
A war within, across life's many stages.

Counseling calls, a beacon dim,
In a world that sees no fault, no grim.
Yet, here I lie, in bed confined,
Seeking solace, yet peace hard to find.

Videos play, a mind to distract,
While fears and worries in shadows react.
What lies ahead, a mystery profound,
In this journey, without solid ground.

But in these whispers of silent despair,
There lies a hope, a breath of air.
To find the strength, the will to rise,
And seek the light beyond the skies.

Though now I feel lost, in darkness confined,
I'll strive to heal, a peace to find.
For within this struggle, a seed does grow,
Of resilience, and a path to follow.

"The real secret of an unsatisfied life lies too often in an unsurrendered will."

- James Hudson Taylor

Perspective

In life's vast canvas, bright hues paint the day,
Yet shadows linger, drawing light away.
We labor with pride, our hearts steady and true,
But words remain, the sting of a harsh review.

In marriage, blessings bloom, quiet yet deep,
A partner's embrace, promises to keep.
Yet we fixate on what's left undone,
Ignoring the warmth of love's gentle sun.

Our families, always present through grief,
Their care a comfort, their love a relief.
Yet, as an only child, cherished yet alone,
I long for a tenderness, a deeper tone.

With siblings close, a burden shared and light,
Yet often, I miss the strength of their sight.
In love, we find both joy and divine,
But focus on flaws, not the souls that align.

The wealthy mourn the peace they cannot claim,
While those with less, dream of fortune's name.
In their pursuit, they fail to see the hands,
That guides them through love's simple strands.

It's time to shift our gaze, our hearts, our mind,
To seek the light, and leave the dark behind.
To honor the good, let gratitude rise,
And see life's beauty, unclouded, with clearer eyes.

"Sometimes the most productive thing you
can do is relax."

- Mark Black

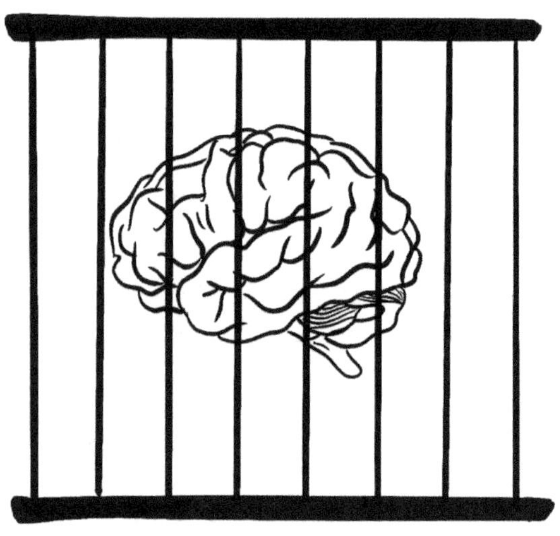

Stresslaxing

In the hushed embrace of the night,
A battle wages out of sight.
Tension tight as twisted string,
As thoughts take flight on a restless wing.

To lay down burdens, ease the mind,
Seems a solace, too hard to find.
For when the work still looms ahead,
Peaceful rest breeds only dread.

The cycle spins, a vicious snare,
Relaxation turns to wear.
Heartbeats drum in frantic sync,
As calm retreats beyond the brink.

Mental turmoil, health decays,
In the labyrinth of endless maze.
Sleepless nights and heavy sighs,
Cloud the clarity of skies.

Traditional ways fall short, alas,
Meditation, a fleeting pass.
Breathing deep, yet gasping still,
As worry breaks through iron will.

But there lies hope, a shift in view,
Force the thoughts to something new.
To seize the now, not fear the past,
A mindful moment, meant to last.

Seek the path where joy resides,
Amidst the chaos, and calm abides.
Step by step, unweave the stress,
In small pursuits, find gentleness.

So break the chains that binds so tight,
Replace the dark with healing light.
For in the grace of letting go,
True peace of mind begins to bloom and grow.

"A happy marriage is a long conversation
which always seems too short."

- André Maurois

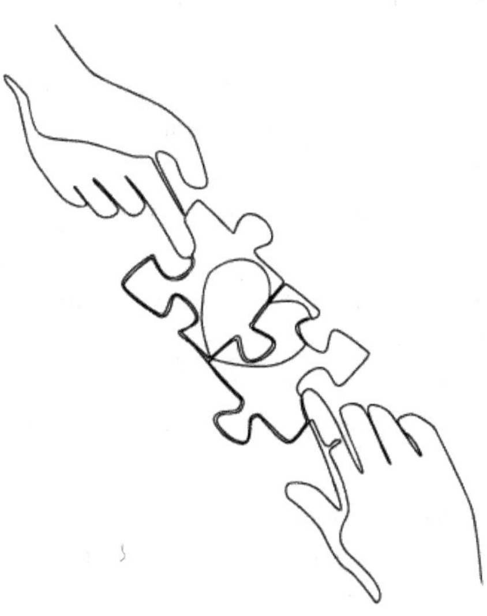

Union

In the land of colors and ancient tales,
An Indian girl embarks on bridal trails.
With hope in her heart, a dream set high,
She seeks a partner, a love to tie.

Through countless faces and many a meet,
Her journey unfolds on this matrimonial street.
The stress of the search, the weight to decide,
A compatible soul, with whom she's aligned.

Parents beside her, with love and doubt,
Guiding her choices, year in, year out.
Negotiables and non-negotiables in play,
Each meeting is a puzzle, by night and by day.

In conversations, she weighs and she learns,
In each hopeful chat, a new spark burns.
Yet anxiety lingers, as prospects,
In the whirlwind of suitors, she's tightly wound.

She tries to enjoy, to smile through the quest,
But it's fast-paced and taxing, a real-life test.
Balancing work, and hobbies she loves,
With the search for a match sent from above.

At last, a compromise, a match that feels right,
Two hearts meet midway, in the soft twilight.
Though not perfect, they decide to unite,
In shared understanding, they find their light.

Through hope and stress, through longing and
tears,
She navigates love, with courage, she steers.
An Indian girl's journey, both modern and old,
In the search for love, her story unfolds.

"Don't be pushed around by the fears in
your mind. Be led by the dreams in your
heart."

– Roy T. Bennett

Awakening

I float through time,
My dreams seem out of rhyme.
Goals I chase, yet they retreat,
As days and nights in battle meet.

Once-clear intentions slowly fade,
Lost in the quiet of night's cascade.
Each moment slips into delay,
And the ticking clock pulls me astray.

I struggle with time's heavy weight,
As doubts grow and hopes dissipate.
The person I thought I'd become,
Feels distant now, like a dream undone.

But in the stillness, something stirs,
A quiet spark that softly spurs.
Strength begins to show,
Guiding me through the undertow.

With this resolve, I start again,
Embracing actions long in vain.
I let go of fear and doubt,
And take the chances calling out.

No longer trapped in hesitation's grasp,
I move with purpose, free at last.
The dreams that seemed so far away,
Are now within my reach today.

Each step I take is a promise made,
To build a future unafraid.
Breaking free from the past's old chain,
I move forward with clear gain.

"A season of loneliness and isolation is
when the caterpillar gets its wings.
Remember that next time you feel alone"

- Mandy Hale

Lonely

In crowded rooms where laughter sings,
A heart alone, in silence clings.
Amidst the smiles and busy throng,
One feels adrift, a note gone wrong.

At bustling cafes, morning's start,
A hollow ache presses the heart.
Conversations ebb and flow,
Yet loneliness begins to grow.

In offices where people strive,
A solitary soul contrives.
To blend, to fit, yet feels apart,
With silent cries from weary heart.

At parties where the joy should soar,
A soul withdrawn still longs for more.
The laughter loud, the music bright,
Can't pierce the cloak of lonely night.

In parks where children laugh and play,
The world seems distant, far away.
A lone observer on the bench,
With thoughts and feelings hard to quench.

The weight of loneliness grows deep,
In silent nights, the tears they weep.
Reflection brings the pain to light,
A yearning for connection's sight.

At first, the heart resists the change,
Afraid of steps that feel so strange.
The fear of judgment, harsh and cold,
Keeps inner warmth from taking hold.

But gently, slowly, courage stirs,
A voice within, a call it purrs.
To reach beyond the comfort zone,
To find that they are not alone.

A book becomes a trusted friend,
In stories, they find hearts to mend.
A walk through nature's calm embrace,
Brings solace in its gentle grace.

In hobbies, passions start to bloom,
Creating space within the gloom.
A painting's stroke, a crafted word,
Gives voice to feelings once unheard.

Reaching out, a trembling hand,
To kindred souls who understand.
In shared experiences, they find,
A balm to soothe the restless mind.

Step by step, the journey's made,
From shadow's grip to sunlight's glade.
With each connection, strong and true,
The lonely heart begins anew.

The progression slow, yet steady, firm,
As self-worth starts to twist and turn.
In learning to befriend the self,
They place their doubts upon the shelf.

And in this growth, a truth reveals,
Through pain, the heart still heals.
For loneliness, though deep and vast,
Can fade away and be surpassed.

Now in those rooms where laughter sings,
The heart no longer, lonely clings.
For in each smile, and every face,
They find their own, their sacred place.

"Whoever lives wins. Don't feel guilty about having survived. If you have time to be feeling guilty, work on living a day longer, a minute longer. And once in a while, remember the ones that died before you. That's good enough."

- Atsuko Asano

Samsara

In the quiet of their twilight years, they sit,
Burdened by a weight too heavy to admit.
Once strong and sure, they now rely,
On younger hands as days go by.

They've walked through life, with heads held high,
Now they struggle, questioning why.
Dependent on those they once raised,
Their worth now feels like a distant phase.

They forget the path they've paved,
The lives they've touched, the love engraved.
The wealth they earned, the home they built,
All now lost in waves of guilt.

They nurtured dreams, they sowed the seed,
Provided all their children need.
With tender care, they shaped each day,
Yet now, in silence, they drift away.

They feel diminished, good for naught,
Lost in a maze of troubled thought.
But they've forgotten, in their pain,
The legacy they leave, the wisdom gained.

Though now they lean, they must recall,
Their strength still holds within it all.
For every choice, every wise decision,
Still guides the family's steady mission.

Even now, their value's clear,
A source of love, of strength, of cheer.
They've given much, they've done it all,
And still, they stand, though they may fall.

So let them see beyond their years,
Beyond the doubts, beyond the fears.
Their worth remains, despite their plight,
A beacon shining ever bright.

In every moment, they're needed still,
For guidance, for wisdom, for love that will.
Continue to nurture, to hold us true,
A family bound by all they do.

"Permit yourself to change your mind when something is no longer working for you."

- Nedra Glover Tawwab

Transition

In the journey of life, where we once stood,
With childhood friends who truly understood.
We thought they'd stay, forever near,
But now they fade, year after year.

The calls grow sparse, the ties grow thin,
They barely ask how we've been.
What once was deep, now feels so light,
A souvenir, a meal - no depth in sight.

Parents now, their roles takes lead,
Their wisdom rooted, their love a seed.
We see their worth in gentler hue,
Just as they always saw in you.

At work, no need for hearts to bind,
A nod, a task—our ties confined.
We neither crave nor feel disdain,
In neutrality, we break the chain.

Being alone no longer stings,
Nor does it make our spirit sing.
A balanced state, not full nor void,
With self-reliance now employed.

Ambition once a raging fire,
Now softer, tempered in desire.
No burning need to chase or race,
We're finding comfort in our pace.

And so we grow, and so we change,
In ways once thought a little strange.
Peace arrives, a quiet tune,
As life unfolds in a calm monsoon.

"Opening the door to self-respect is a key of happiness."

— Charles Glassman

Waves

There's a hush in the room, you're not here,
A hollow space devours the air.
I sit, unmoved, in the soft haze of time,
And all feel distant, unclear, unfair.

The clock ticks, it doesn't speak to me,
The hours are endless waves at sea.
Lethargy becomes my closest friend,
And in the crowd, I'm still alone, you see.

I could reach out, but I fall back,
The words to others feel heavy, slack.
No company cures the ache inside,
When the heart chooses to hide.

But slowly, like dawn after endless night,
I find a spark, a flicker of light.
In quiet moments, I turn to the self,
Rediscovering the joy of solitude's wealth.

Work and hobbies hum a gentle tune,
The days begin not to drag too soon.
I build a rhythm, a place that's all mine,
Emotionally stable, I start to feel fine.

But then, the door swings, you appear,
And with you comes a familiar fear.
I've found peace in my steady way,
Yet here I am, swaying, come what may.

I give, I bend, though I feel the strain,
Knowing you'll leave, and I'll face it again.
The cycle repeats, and loneliness returns,
A lesson in love, as the heart still yearns.

And so I learn to walk this fragile line,
Not far from you, but keeping me in mind.
Loneliness is a shadow we all must bear,
But balance is the way we care.

I love you, but I'll love me too,
In places where hurt can't seep through.
For life will ebb, and loved ones will roam,
But I'll find my center, my heart, my home.

"Being nervous isn't bad, it means something important is happening."

- Joseph Chilton Pearce

Embrace

Fear has faces, both shadow and guide,
It suffocates or helps you decide.
Some call it poison, a thief of the soul,
A force that turns clarity into a hole.

It makes the world feel frail,
The more you yield, the more you derail.
But others call fear a keeper, a friend,
A voice that warns, guides till the end.

It tempers the reckless, keeps us aligned,
Offering balance, protecting the mind.
Fears must be faced to sever the chains,
Phobias bind us, like floods and flames.

Conquering these shadows demands a fight,
Overcoming fear, we reclaim the light.
Without confrontation, we remain in the past,
Frozen in time, too afraid to move fast.

Fear, a burden, teacher, truth we must trust,
A mirror, a compass, to help us adjust.
We have our battles, a unique road to tread,
Either confront it or let it recede instead.

In fear's quiet dance, we find ourselves grow,
While facing them, that we truly know.
Fear, not an enemy, but a force to respect,
A partner in growth, when we pause to reflect.

"Obstacles can't stop you. Problems can't stop you. Most of all, other people can't stop you. Only you can stop you.
Let failure do not discourage you to keep going in your efforts. No one can stop you without your permission!"

- Jeffrey Gitomer

Labyrinth

I send my hopes adrift in a digital stream,
Each click a wish, each line a dream.
My inbox, silent, a hollow tune,
The sun sets, rises, and sets too soon.

Hundreds of doors, I knock and plead,
A forest of "No," where my dreams recede.
The weight of rejections, heavy to bear,
Yet hope, a flicker, lingers somewhere.

At my desk, where the hours crawl,
Beneath the weight of a corporate thrall.
Tasks unending, my spirit confined,
Yet bound by the chains of bills aligned.

Interviews arrive, a moment's grace,
Then falter, dissolve, a familiar place.
"Not the right fit," they often decree,
As doubt's cold shadow envelops me.

A bad boss once, a toxic sea,
I pray the next won't mirror thee.
But fear sits heavy, a lurking guest,
Will this leap lead to earned rest?

Firms sift piles with hurried hands,
Shortlists formed from shifting sands.
In haste, they miss what's best and true,
While gems are lost in the endless queue.

And all the while, society stares,
Judges my worth by the job I bear.
A title, a paycheck, the company's name,
My life reduced to a shallow frame.

Oh, this hunt, this ceaseless grind,
A test of patience, a trial of mind.
Yet through it all, I hold my ground,
For someday, somewhere, I'll be found.

"The greatest thing you'll ever learn is just
to love and be loved in return."

– Eden Ahbez

Unravelled

In masks and hurried days,
Truths are cloaked in shadowed haze.
Love treads softly, seeking ground,
But finds no space, no room unbound.

We carry burdens, shoulders bent,
Chasing dreams, our lives are spent.
A market's roar, a proving game,
Our hearts for sale, yet none to claim.

On screens we shine, smiles we mold,
Hide timid stories, truths untold.
An endless scroll, a fleeting glance,
What remains for love to dance?

With choices, yet hearts grow cold,
Afraid to risk, too scared to hold.
Vulnerability, a fragile art,
A risk too great for guarded hearts.

But love persists, a stubborn light,
Through tangled webs, endless night.
It whispers soft, it waits unseen,
In moments raw, in spaces clean.

Not in the market's clamor loud,
Nor in the scroll of fleeting crowd.
But in the gaze where fears dissolve,
In shared resolve, love will evolve.

Let go the weight, the proving guise,
Let tears unveil the guarded eyes.
Love is neither bought nor sold,
It blooms where hearts grow brave and bold.

"Sometimes the hardest part isn't letting go
but learning to start over."

– Nicole Sobon

Heal

I thought I moved on from the past,
Yet its weight in my chest clings fast.
It sneaks back in, a whisper of wrong,
And I ponder if peace will ever belong.

I wear a smile, yet feel a sting,
A shadow where light ought to spring.
My heart feels split, a rift so wide,
Torn 'twixt what was and what must abide.

With each step forward, I think I've triumphed,
Yet fear trips me up, my spirit defunct.
Like a storm that remains, but never quite swells,
A wound that lingers, a tale it retells.

I thought that the ache would fade into air,
Yet with each dawn, it finds me in despair.
I question if ever, I'll reach a resolve,
For the echoes of sorrow refuse to dissolve.

At times, it feels like I'm utterly still,
Then suddenly swept by a tempest of will.
I'm striving to heal, to reshape my fate,
But the hurt finds its home, a place to await.

I tell myself that I possess might,
That in time, my spirit will reunite.
Yet in silence, a shadow treads deep,
A truth beneath pain that rouses my sleep.

Fear and doubt are like waves that crest,
Leaving me drowning in questions unguessed.
I try to inhale, let my troubles flow,
But wonder if I'll ever stand tall, unbowed.

Healing's not what I once perceived,
Not a straight road, nor a goal to be achieved.
It's a dance between love and the loss that I feel,
A truth in my heart that I strive to conceal.

So I carry both joy and grief in my hands,
Walking through days with their shifting sands.
Trying to trust in the hope I yearn,
That someday, at last, I will truly learn.

"Life is what happens when you're busy
making other plans."

– John Lennon

Living

In the gentle mornings of times gone by,
When the sunlight spilled softly in the sky.
And the day didn't rush in a hurry,
We awakened, hearts unfettered, like birds in a
flurry.

Do you recall those mornings, that tender
embrace?
When the world's weight didn't pull at your grace.
Each moment seemed to flow with an effortless
sway,
A simple rhythm, perfect in every way.

But time, like a river, began to pull fast,
Bringing along with it a tide that wouldn't last.
The world grew hectic, moments slipped past,
We stood in the current, feeling so outclassed.

The hours stretched thin, the days seemed to race,
Our hearts once buoyant, now feel the pressure's
trace.
Chasing after dreams, we lost our place,
In that frantic pursuit, we couldn't keep pace.

Work seeped in like an unbidden guest,
Pressing down with its constant request.
We gave our all, but found no rest,
The joys of our lives, we couldn't digest.

With each passing day, the toll started to show,
Our bodies, once vibrant, now weary and low.
What was once health became a battle, a woe,
And in our longing for peace, we forgot how to
grow.

Fitness whispers, but it's weighed by the strife,
Amidst the clamor, it's hard to find life.
We run and we fight, yet still we seek rest,
A quiet moment, a soothing chest.

In this realm, where the noise takes its throne,
We've crafted lives that feel just overthrown.
But deep within us, in the stillness, we've known,
That truth will return, with lessons to be shown.

I see you caught up in this relentless race,
Yearning for a sanctuary, a peaceful space.
A life where balance and love find their place,
Where joy isn't fleeting but remains with grace.